Roar of ‘Ēzer

Christian A. Dickinson

Title: *Roar of 'Ēzer*
Subtitle: *Reclaiming God's Vision for Women's Strength and Partnership*
Written by: Christian A. Dickinson
Illustrations by: Learning Engineered LLC
Published by: Learning Engineered Publishing

Library of Congress Control Number: 2025943019
ISBN (Print): 978-1-965741-41-2

First Edition: 2025

Printed & Created in: United States of America
Text and Illustration Copyright © 2025

Learning Engineered Publishing is a division of Learning Engineered LLC and a subsidiary of Carpe Diem Unlimited Holdings, Inc.

LEARNING ENGINEERED
PUBLISHING

Contents

Dedication

To my daughters, Darcy, Abigayle, and Amelia—may you always embrace the fierce, God-given strength of your ʻēzer and let it roar.

To their future husbands—may you honor and champion the warriors beside you.

To Morgan, my ʻēzer and partner—your courage inspires this story and our life together.

And to every reader—may you rise in the harmony of God's design, reflecting His image with boldness and love.

Preface

This book began in a quiet moment—reading stories to my daughter Darcy, her eyes wide with wonder—only to notice how often those tales dimmed the strength God wove into girls. I wasn't a writer; I was an engineer, trained to design systems that work. So I set out to build a truer story—one that reflected God's blueprint for women.

That search led me from children's books to devotionals, and finally to Scripture itself, where one word roared to life: *'ēzer*. In Genesis, God calls woman *'ēzer kenegdo*—not a mere helper, but a rescuing strength, a warrior beside man, the same term He uses for Himself as Israel's defender. This truth didn't just challenge my as-sumptions; it rebuilt them. It healed something in me, too.

It transformed my marriage. What started as a project became a testimony. When Morgan, my *'ēzer*, and I embraced this calling together—two image-bearers reflecting God's likeness—it was like a lion awakening in our home. Her roar doesn't make me shrink; it calls me to rise, in awe of who she was created to be.

In these pages, you'll find stories, reflections, and a journey through Scripture that uncovers God's design for women—fierce, purposeful, and free. This book is for my daughters, so they never doubt their God-given strength. It's for their future husbands, to honor that strength without fear. And it's for Morgan, my partner and warrior, whose courage has made me a better man, husband, and father.

May this book stir you to let your *'ēzer* roar—to rise and live the story you were made for.

Introduction-The Word That Changes Everything

"It is not good for the man to be alone. I will make a helper suitable for him." — Genesis 2:18

For too long, we've heard "helper" and thought less.
Less than the man. Less than equal. Less than essential.

We've pictured a woman in the shadows—supportive, sure, but secondary.
An assistant to the man's mission. A quiet echo to his voice.

But what if "helper" is no small word?
What if it's a divine declaration of strength, purpose, and partnership?

In Hebrew, the word is *'ēzer*.

And it's not soft. It's not subservient.

It's the word Scripture uses for God Himself—fierce, rescuing, life-giving.

> **"The Lord is my help and my shield." — Psalm 33:20**

> **"You ride the heavens to my help, O God." — Deuteronomy 33:26**

When God called the woman *'ēzer*, He didn't make her a sidekick.

He made her a warrior.

A vital counterpart.

The one who completes the reflection of His image alongside the man.

She wasn't an afterthought.

She was the answer to creation's first "not good."

This book is a journey to reclaim *'ēzer*—
to strip away centuries of small, cultural as-
sumptions
and rediscover the woman's God-given
strength, wisdom, and purpose.

It's for women who've been told they're "just
helpers,"
and for men ready to honor the power beside
them.

It's for anyone longing to see God's design for
men and women
not as hierarchy, but as harmony.

In these pages, we'll trace *'ēzer* through Scripture—
from Eden's garden to Jesus' radical inclusion of
women.

We'll uncover how sin distorted this divine word
and how Christ began its restoration.

We'll see why getting *'ēzer* right reshapes everything—

our relationships, our churches, and the gospel of the Kingdom.

It's time to stop shrinking the word God spoke over women.
It's time to let *'ēzer* roar.

Chapter 1
The First "Not Good"

In the beginning, everything sang with goodness.

Light spilled across the void—good.
Seas carved their boundaries, land bloomed with life—good.
Stars blazed, birds soared, beasts roamed—good.
Then God formed man from dust, breathing life into his frame—good.

But in the heart of Eden, amid paradise's perfection, God paused.
For the first time, something wasn't good.

"Then the Lord God said, 'It is not good for the man to be alone. I will

make a helper suitable for him."
— Genesis 2:18

This wasn't about sin.
It wasn't a flaw in creation.
It was about solitude.

Adam wasn't idle.
He named the animals, tended the garden, and walked with God in the evening breeze.
Yet, surrounded by beauty and purpose, he was incomplete.

Alone, he could not fully reflect the image of a God
who exists in eternal communion—Father, Son, Spirit.

> **"Let Us make mankind in Our image... male and female He created them." — Genesis 1:26–27**

God's image shines brightest not in man alone,
nor in woman alone,
but in their unity.

Without her, something divine was missing.

So God orchestrated a moment of revelation.
He paraded the animals before Adam—lion
with lioness, eagle with mate—
each a pair, a counterpart.

Adam named them, but as he did, a truth settled in his heart:
he had no match.

> **"But for Adam, no suitable helper
> was found." — Genesis 2:20**

Then God acted.
He cast Adam into a deep sleep, reached into
his side—
not his head to dominate her,
not his feet to trample her,

but his rib, close to his heart—
and crafted the woman.

When Adam awoke, his voice broke the silence
with awe:

> **"This at last is bone of my bones
> and flesh of my flesh!" — Genesis
> 2:23**

Not servant. Not subordinate.
His equal. His reflection. His partner—
flesh of his flesh, yet gloriously distinct.

Before she spoke a word, God had already de-
clared her worth.
She was the answer to the first "not good."
She was the crescendo of creation.
She was *'ēzer*.

The Word That Redefines Everything

The Hebrew word *'ēzer* isn't what we've often
made it.

We hear "helper" and think of an assistant fetching tools,
a sidekick trailing behind.

We picture a teacher's aide—not the teacher;
a supporter—not the star.

But Scripture doesn't play small with *'ēzer*.
It's the word for God Himself when He storms into battle for His people.

> **"You are my help and my deliver-er, O Lord." — Psalm 70:5**

'ēzer is strength.
'ēzer is rescue.
'ēzer is a force that turns the tide.

Paired with *kenegdo*—"corresponding to him, equal to him"—
it paints a picture of a woman who stands face-to-face with man,
perfectly matched, opposite in form, yet united in purpose.

'ēzer kenegdo:
a vital partner, a strength-giver,
the one without whom creation could not be complete.

This isn't hierarchy. It's harmony.
This isn't weakness. It's mutuality.
This isn't an intern. It's a savior.

Why This Matters Now

Misreading *'ēzer* doesn't just skew Genesis—it ripples into our lives.

When we call women "just helpers," we dim their God-given light
and distort men's vision of partnership.

We've seen it in churches where women's voices are silenced,
in homes where mutuality is mistaken for control,
in hearts where women doubt their worth.

But when we reclaim *'ēzer*, we begin to see clearly.

The woman was never an afterthought—
she was God's intentional answer.

She wasn't created to follow in the shadows—
but to stand side by side,
reflecting the glory of God together with man.

In the next chapter, we'll trace *'ēzer* through
Scripture—
from the Psalms to the prophets—
and uncover why this one word holds the key
to understanding God's heart for women—
and for us all.

Chapter 2
The Echo of God's Strength

The woman in Eden wasn't just a partner—she was *'ēzer kenegdo*,
a strength beside the man,
woven from his side
to reflect God's image.

That single verse in Genesis 2:18 wasn't a fleeting note in creation's song.
It was a chord struck deep,
resonating with the very name God claims for Himself.

To hear its full harmony,
we must trace *'ēzer* through Scripture's pages.

What we find isn't soft or secondary.
It's seismic.

God as 'Ezer: The Rescuer Who Thunders

The Hebrew word *'ēzer* appears twenty-one
times in the Old Testament.
Sixteen of those point to God—
not as a quiet supporter,
but as a warrior who shatters the impossible.

Picture Israel, trembling before enemies,
their backs against the sea.
God doesn't send an assistant.
He parts the waters.

> **"Blessed are you, Israel! Who is
> like you, a people saved by the
> Lord? He is your shield and helper
> ('ēzer), your glorious sword." —
> Deuteronomy 33:29**

Or David, hunted by Saul, hiding in caves, his
heart pounding.
He cries:

"Our soul waits for the Lord; He is our help ('ēzer) and our shield." — Psalm 33:20

This isn't help with daily tasks.
This is divine deliverance—
the kind that rewrites fates.

God is *'ēzer* when Pharaoh's chariots close in.
God is *'ēzer* when hope is a flicker in the dark.

"You are my help ('ēzer) and my deliverer, O Lord—do not delay!" — Psalm 70:5

Here, *'ēzer* is urgent,
tied to life-or-death rescue,
a cry for the One who arrives with thunder.

This is the word God chose for the woman in Eden.
Not subordinate.
Not sidelined.
A force.

A rescuer.
A reflection of His own might.

The Pulse of 'Ezer: Power in Crisis

'ēzer isn't a casual word—
it's born in battle.

When Moses names his son Eliezer—"My God is Help"—
he's not marking a minor favor.
He's honoring the God who saved him from Pharaoh's sword.

> **"My father's God was my helper ('ēzer); he saved me from the sword of Pharaoh." — Exodus 18:4**

'ēzer is a victory cry.

In Psalm 89:19, God declares:

"I have bestowed help ('ēzer) on one who is mighty."

Here, *'ēzer* empowers a king for battle—
not as a crutch,
but as a crown.

Even in its rare non-divine uses—like allies aid-
ing Israel in war (Isaiah 30:5)—
'ēzer carries weight,
implying strength that shifts the tide.

Every time *'ēzer* appears, it pulses with purpose:
Power alongside presence.
Rescue woven with resolve.

When God named the woman *'ēzer*,
He wasn't echoing the man's need.
He was echoing His own name.

The Lie We've Believed

Let's be honest.
The word "helper" trips us up.

In our world, it's a demotion:
"She's just my helper."
"He's only helping out."

We hear "assistant"
and picture someone fetching coffee—
not forging history.

But Scripture doesn't play that game.
God as *'ēzer* doesn't fetch tools—He fells giants.
The woman as *'ēzer* doesn't trail behind—she
stands as the strength creation craved.

There's a chasm between help that serves hierarchy
and help that saves humanity.

God is *'ēzer* because no one else can do what He
does.
The woman is *'ēzer* for the same reason—
because without her, God's mission falters.

Kenegdo: The Strength of Face-to-Face

The word *kenegdo* sharpens this vision.
"Corresponding to him."
"Equal in essence."
"Opposite, yet matched."

She wasn't formed from Adam's head to rule over him.
Nor from his feet, to be trampled beneath him.
But from his side—
bone of his bone,
heart beside heart.

'ēzer kenegdo isn't about roles or rank.
It's about unity—
two distinct flames, burning as one for God's purpose.

In Genesis, the man was incomplete,
not because he was weak,
but because God's image demands both—
male and female, side by side.

This isn't a chain of command.
It's a dance of creation.

Why This Shifts Everything

Calling the woman *'ēzer* wasn't a footnote in Eden—
it was a revelation.

She wasn't a patch for loneliness.
She was a pillar for God's glory.

Her strength isn't a threat—
it's a mirror of the God who saves.

The same word that named her in creation's dawn
named God in Israel's darkest nights.

Let that truth breathe:
The woman carries the strength of the Divine.

Yet we've dimmed this light—
in churches where women's voices are hushed,
in homes where partnership bends toward power,
in hearts where women doubt their calling.

When we shrink *'ēzer*,
we don't just shrink womanhood—
we shrink God's image.

But when we reclaim it, we see clearly:
Her presence isn't optional—it's ordained.
Her power isn't peripheral—it's prophetic.

A Glimpse Beyond the Garden

The echo of *'ēzer* doesn't end in the Old Testament.

When Jesus lifts women to learn at His feet
(Luke 10:39),
or entrusts a Samaritan woman to proclaim His
truth (John 4:39),
He's restoring what Eden began.

'ēzer isn't just a Hebrew word—
it's a kingdom calling,
pulsing through every woman who rises to deliver, teach, and heal.

In the next chapter, we'll meet these
women—Scripture's fiercest *'ēzers*.

From Deborah, wielding justice on the battlefield,
to Priscilla, shaping the early church—
they didn't just help.
They saved.

They weren't defying God's design.
They were declaring it.
And so can we.

Chapter 3
Fierce ʿĒzers: Women Who Delivered

The woman in Eden was named *ʿēzer keneg-do*—
a strength, a rescuer,
a reflection of God's own might.

Chapter Two showed us *ʿēzer* echoing through Scripture,
a word of power God claims for Himself.

Now, we meet the women who lived it.
They didn't just help.
They delivered.

From battlefields to house churches,
they rose as *ʿēzers*—
warriors of God's design,
saving, leading, reshaping history.

Their stories aren't exceptions.
They're revelations.

Deborah: The Judge Who Waged Victory

Deborah didn't wait in the shadows.
A prophetess and judge,
she sat beneath a palm tree,
wielding wisdom over Israel.

> **"Deborah, a prophetess... was leading Israel at that time."** — **Judges 4:4–5**

When God's people faced Sisera's iron chariots,
she summoned Barak and declared:

> **"The Lord will deliver them into your hand."** — **Judges 4:7**

Barak hesitated.
Deborah didn't.

She marched to battle—
her voice a divine trumpet,
her leadership the turning point of the war.

When Sisera fled, another *'ēzer*, Jael,
drove a tent peg through his skull (Judges 4:21).

Together, they crushed oppression.

Deborah was *'ēzer*—
not as a servant, but as a leader.
Her strength turned the tide.

Her song in Judges 5 thunders with praise,
not for playing small,
but for partnering with God to save.

Esther: The Queen Who Risked Everything

Esther stood at a crossroads of annihilation.
Her people faced Haman's plot—
a genocide sealed with the king's signet ring
(Esther 3:13).

An orphan turned queen,
she could have stayed silent,
hidden behind palace walls.

Instead, she fasted, prayed,
and stepped into the king's court—uninvited,
risking her life.

"If I perish, I perish." — Esther 4:16

Her courage wasn't passive.
It was *'ēzer* in action—
a calculated strike against evil.

Through her, God delivered a nation.

Esther wasn't a sidekick to Mordecai's plan.
She was the pivot,
her strength echoing God's rescue in Exodus.

Priscilla: The Teacher Who Built the Church

In the New Testament,
Priscilla steps forward—

no longer bound by Eden's shadow,
but radiant in Christ's restoration.

With her husband Aquila,
she taught Apollos—
a gifted preacher—
the fuller truth of the gospel.

**"She and Aquila took him aside
and explained to him the way
of God more accurately." — Acts
18:26**

She didn't whisper corrections.
She instructed.
Her voice shaped the early church.

Paul calls her a co-worker, not a subordinate
(Romans 16:3).

Priscilla was *'ēzer kenegdo*—
standing face-to-face with her husband,
her wisdom fortifying the mission.

Her strength wasn't a threat.
It was a cornerstone.

The Design Declared

These women weren't breaking God's mold.
They were fulfilling it.

Deborah's justice.
Esther's courage.
Priscilla's teaching.

Each one reflects the *'ēzer*
who storms into battle,
who saves from destruction,
who builds God's kingdom.

Yet for centuries, we've told women to shrink.
To serve quietly.
To doubt their fire.

No more.

Their stories shout what Genesis whispered:
Women's strength is God's image unleashed.

In churches, in homes, in hearts—
we need *'ēzers* to rise.
Not as assistants.
As deliverers.

In the next chapter,
we'll explore how sin twisted this divine design—
and how Jesus began restoring it.
Calling women to rise again.
Calling them to roar.

Chapter 4
The Fall and the Fracture

In Eden, man and woman stood side by side—
unashamed, unbroken, unafraid.

He, formed from the dust.
She, formed from his side.

Together, *'ēzer kenegdo*—strength matched with strength.
Different, yet one.
Harmony, not hierarchy.

And then something cracked.

> **"You will be like God," the serpent said. — Genesis 3:5**

With that lie, the unraveling began.

Sin Didn't Create Roles—It Corrupted Relationship

In the moment of temptation, Satan didn't approach the man and woman together.
He spoke to the woman, not because she was weaker—
but because dividing them was the strategy.

He planted suspicion.
He reframed God's command as control.
And the woman reached.

> **"She took of its fruit and ate; and she also gave some to her husband, who was with her." — Genesis 3:6**

The man was silent.
The woman acted.
And both fell.

The immediate consequence wasn't just guilt.
It was separation.

From God.
From each other.
From the design that had once danced in unity.

And then came the words that echoed across millennia.

> **"Your desire will be for your husband, and he will rule over you."**
> **— Genesis 3:16**

The Curse Was Never the Calling

This verse has often been mistaken for instruction.
But God wasn't commanding hierarchy—
He was describing the consequence of sin.

The Fall didn't introduce a godly structure.
It fractured a holy partnership.

Where once there was mutuality, now there would be control.
Where once there was strength beside strength, now there would be a struggle for power.

The woman would long to restore intimacy, but the man would grasp for dominance.

This wasn't design.
This was damage.

Patriarchy: A Symptom of the Fall

From that moment on, the distortion spread.

Cain killed his brother.
Lamech sang songs of violence.
Nimrod built empires and named himself mighty.

Men ruled not as image-bearers, but as conquerors.

Women were silenced, traded, forgotten.

Even God's own people reflected this broken-
ness:
Polygamy.
Power plays.
Generational sin.

But if we mistake these stories as prescriptions
instead of warnings,
we become complicit in the fracture.

God didn't approve of the broken systems—He
worked through them
to preserve the promise of restoration.

He didn't abandon *'ēzer*—He hid it like a seed,
waiting for the right time to bloom again.

Jesus and the Beginning of Restoration

And then... Jesus came.

Born of a woman.
Announced by a woman.
Followed by women.
Resurrected to a woman.

Everywhere He walked, He turned the curse upside down.

He spoke to the Samaritan woman in broad daylight (John 4).
He allowed Mary to sit at His feet like a disciple (Luke 10).
He healed, dignified, and defended.
He welcomed women into the center of the story.

He didn't reinforce the fracture.
He began to heal it.

Redeemed, Not Rewritten

Jesus didn't erase the distinction between male and female.
He redeemed their design.

He didn't call the woman to become the man, nor the man to overpower the woman.

He called both to submit to one another out of reverence for Christ (Ephesians 5:21).

The Cross didn't flatten gender—
it restored partnership.

The church was birthed in an upper room with
men and women together.
The Spirit fell on both sons and daughters (Acts
2:17).

The new creation had begun—
not in sameness,
but in unity of purpose.

Why It Matters

If the Fall introduced the fracture,
then Christ invites us to repair it.

But that only happens when we stop mistaking
the curse for the design.

The woman wasn't made to be ruled.
She was made to reign with.

The man wasn't made to dominate.
He was made to dwell alongside.

Until we see that,
we'll keep confusing submission with silence,
and leadership with control.

But when we reclaim Eden's vision,
when we see *'ēzer* through the lens of the Cross,
we begin to rebuild what was lost.

Side by side.
Strength beside strength.

In the next chapter,
we'll walk deeper into the life and ministry of
Jesus—
and see how He didn't just restore *'ēzer*—
He released it.

Chapter 5
Jesus and the 'Ēzer Released

Jesus Released 'Ēzer

In Eden, *'ēzer kenegdo* named the woman as strength, God's image-bearer alongside man.

Chapter 3 showed women like Deborah and Priscilla living this truth.
But sin fractured the design, casting women into shadows.

Then Jesus came—born of a woman, announced by a woman, witnessed by women.
He didn't just restore *'ēzer*.
He released it.

His ministry and resurrection unleashed women as partners, proclaimers, and pillars of the kingdom.

Honored in Ministry: Women at the Center

Jesus didn't sideline women—He centered them.

The Samaritan woman at the well wasn't a by-stander; she was a herald.
"Come, see a man who told me everything I ever did," she proclaimed, drawing her city to Christ (John 4:39).
Her voice, once marginalized, became *'ēzer*—a strength that delivered truth.

Mary of Bethany sat at His feet, a disciple's place, defying cultural norms.
"Mary has chosen what is better," Jesus declared (Luke 10:42).
He honored her learning, her *'ēzer* mind, as equal to any man's.

The bleeding woman, unclean for twelve years, reached for His cloak.
Jesus didn't recoil—He called her *"daughter"* and healed her (Mark 5:34).
Her faith, her *'ēzer* courage, was a testimony to God's power.

These women weren't accessories.
They were essential, their strength woven into Jesus' mission.

Exalted at the Resurrection: First Witnesses

When the world turned dark at the cross, women stayed.

Mary Magdalene, Mary the mother of James, and others stood vigil, their *'ēzer* resolve unshaken (Matthew 27:55–56).

When Jesus rose, He didn't appear to Peter or John first.
He chose Mary Magdalene, a woman once demon-possessed, to carry the greatest news:
"I have seen the Lord!" (John 20:18).

She wasn't a footnote—she was the first apostle of the resurrection.

This was no accident.

Jesus entrusted women to proclaim the victory that shattered death, affirming their *'ēzer* calling as deliverers of God's truth.

A Kingdom Restored

Jesus didn't erase male and female—He redeemed their partnership.

When the Spirit fell at Pentecost, it was on *"sons and daughters"* alike (Acts 2:17).
Women prophesied, prayed, and led, their voices echoing Joel's promise.

Jesus' actions weren't cultural concessions—they were a return to Eden's design: strength beside strength, *'ēzer kenegdo* unleashed.

Yet the world resists.
Even today, some churches dim women's light,
mistaking the Fall's fracture for God's plan.

Jesus shows us otherwise.

He honored women as disciples, healers, proclaimers—co-burden bearers of His kingdom.

The Call Forward

The *'ēzer* vision isn't a relic.
It's a revolution.

Jesus released women to be strength-bearers,
not shadows.

In the next chapter, we'll see how sin tried to
bury this truth—
and how we can reclaim it, restoring God's design in our world.

Chapter 6
Living 'Ēzer Today: Strength Unleashed

The woman was named *'ēzer kenegdo—*
God's strength in human form,
a partner reflecting His image.

From Eden's dawn to Deborah's battlefield,
Esther's courage to Priscilla's teaching,
we've seen *'ēzers* rise as deliverers.

In the last chapter, we watched Jesus
restore what sin distorted—
lifting women to proclaim resurrection,
to disciple, to lead,
to stand as strength beside strength again.

Now the call echoes to us.

This is not ancient theology.
This is a present-tense invitation.

What does it mean to live as *'ēzer* today?

'Ēzer in the Church: Voices That Shape

Scripture's *'ēzers* didn't whisper—they led.
Yet too often today, women's voices are muted in pews and pulpits.

But Paul wrote:

> **"There is neither male nor female, for you are all one in Christ Jesus."**
> **— Galatians 3:28**

This wasn't a call to erase difference.
It was a call to unleash unity.

Phoebe, a deacon, carried and likely read Paul's letter to the Romans (Romans 16:1–2).
Priscilla taught Apollos the fullness of the gospel (Acts 18:26).
Junia was *"outstanding among the apostles."* (Romans 16:7)

These are not side characters.
They are *'ēzers*—strength-bearing leaders in the early Church.

When women are silenced,
half the image of God is restrained.

But when their gifts are welcomed—
preaching like Deborah, mentoring like Priscilla,
serving like Phoebe—
the Church breathes more fully.

'Ēzer strength doesn't divide the body.
It completes it.

'Ēzer in the Home: Partnership, Not Power

In the home, *'ēzer* redefines marriage and family.
Kenegdo means *"face-to-face"*—
equal in essence, united in purpose.

But culture has often cast women as subordinates
and men as unquestioned authorities.

Scripture tells a different story:

> **"Husbands, love your wives, just as Christ loved the church and gave Himself up for her." — Ephesians 5:25**

Love does not dominate.
Love lays down power to lift up partnership.

An *'ēzer* wife isn't a silent supporter—
she's a co-warrior,
fighting for joy, justice, and generational blessing.

Mothers, sisters, daughters—
their strength forms the heart of a family.
Their voice shapes sons and daughters
who walk in truth and courage.

The home is not the man's to rule.
It is the couple's to steward—together.

'Ēzer in the World: Courage That Transforms

Beyond church and home,
'ēzers rise in classrooms, courtrooms, clinics, and corporations.

Like Jael driving the peg (Judges 4:21), modern women confront injustice head-on.

They mentor at-risk youth.
They fight human trafficking.
They lead with wisdom and compassion in boardrooms and nonprofits.

Their strength is not rebellion.
It is rescue.

Yet the world often mistrusts bold women—labeling them bossy, emotional, or threatening.

But Psalm 68:11 declares:

> **"The Lord gives the word; the women who proclaim it are a mighty throng."**

'Ēzers are not the exception.
They are the evidence
that God is still saving, still delivering, still calling.

Every act of justice, every word of truth,
every quiet decision to do what is right—
this is 'ēzer unleashed in the world.

The Call to Rise

Being 'ēzer is not about striving.
It is about stepping into the name God already
spoke over you.

Women—
Your voice is not too loud.
Your wisdom is not too much.
Your presence is not a threat.
It's a revelation.

You are not an echo.
You are an answer.
You are 'ēzer—rescuer, strength-bearer,
crafted in God's image to stand face-to-face

with man,
declaring His glory in every sphere.

Men—
You were never called to dominate,
but to honor the *'ēzer* beside you,
as Adam did when he said in awe:
"This at last is bone of my bone."

When we walk side by side,
not in hierarchy but in harmony,
we reflect the Triune God who made us.

The world needs *'ēzers* now—
not tomorrow, not when it's comfortable,
but now.

Rise, *'ēzer*.
Your strength was never meant to be silent.
It was meant to roar.

Chapter 7
A Kingdom Reshaped: The 'Ēzer Vision Unleashed

From Eden's first breath,
God named the woman *'ēzer kenegdo*—
rescuer, strength-bearer,
equal partner in His image.

We've traced this name through Scripture:
from the garden to the battlefield,
from prophetic voices to resurrection mornings.

We've seen Jesus restore what the Fall fractured—
unleashing women to lead, teach, proclaim,
and heal.

In the last chapter, we saw what it means to live
as *'ēzer*
in our homes, churches, and communities.

But what happens when we stop resisting that vision?
What happens when *'ēzer* is unleashed—
not just personally, but globally?

Everything changes.

Relationships Restored: Harmony Over Hierarchy

God's design for man and woman was never about power.
It was about partnership.

In Eden, they stood side by side—
not in competition,
but in communion.

When we reclaim *'ēzer kenegdo*,
marriages become mutual.
Friendships become fearless.
Families become places of safety and strength.

Peter wrote:

"Husbands, in the same way be considerate as you live with your wives, and treat them with respect as co-heirs of the gracious gift of life." — 1 Peter 3:7

Not helpers and heads.
Co-heirs.

This is what happens when we stop viewing
God's design
as a hierarchy to protect
and start seeing it as a dance to join.

When we honor women as *'ēzer*,
men flourish too.

Because strength beside strength doesn't diminish one—
it elevates both.

Churches Revived: The Spirit's Full Voice

The Church is starved for strength.
Not the strength of control,

but the strength of Christ—
serving, teaching, lifting others higher.

And half that strength has too often been silenced.

But revival is never partial.
It doesn't come through half the Body of Christ.
It comes when sons and daughters prophesy.

Joel's words were clear:

> **"I will pour out My Spirit on all people. Your sons and daughters will prophesy." — Joel 2:28**

On Pentecost, the Spirit fell on both—
and the Church was born through equality, not exclusion.

When we welcome *'ēzer* gifts,
we unlock the full breath of the Spirit.

Women preaching, leading, discipling, worshiping—

not as exceptions,
but as expressions of Eden restored.

Imagine the Church where every Deborah rises.
Where every Priscilla equips.
Where every Mary of Magdala proclaims.

This is not theological compromise.
This is revival.

The Kingdom Breaking In: Culture Transformed

Beyond sanctuaries and households,
'ēzer transforms the world.

In every place where injustice reigns—
God sends rescuers.

In every system that oppresses—
God raises *'ēzers* to dismantle it.

Esther confronted genocide.
Jael shattered tyranny.

Today's *'ēzers* lead revolutions in classrooms,
courtrooms, and clinics.

Psalm 68:11 says:

> **"The Lord gives the word; the women who proclaim it are a mighty throng."**

That word wasn't just for ancient Israel.
It's for now.

It's for women standing at border crossings,
in battered women's shelters,
in legislative chambers,
in hospital rooms,
in refugee camps.

Their voices carry the Kingdom.

And when men stand beside them,
not blocking their roar, but amplifying it—
we get a glimpse of heaven on earth.

This isn't just about gender.
It's about glory.

When we unleash the *'ēzer* vision,
we begin to see what God always intended—
not domination,
but healing.
Not silence,
but symphony.

The Call to Begin

This is not the end of the story.
It's the invitation to join it.

Women—
Your strength is not rebellion.
It is redemption in motion.

Speak.
Lead.
Build.
Prophesy.

You are not waiting for permission.
God already called you by name: *'ēzer*.

Men—
Your calling is not to control.

It is to co-labor.
To protect, not possess.
To honor, not hover.
To rejoice when she rises.

Because her rise does not threaten yours—
it fulfills it.

Churches—
Stop guarding your pulpits from God's daughters.
Open them.

Revival will not come through silencing His image.
It will come when you let *'ēzer* roar.

Families. Schools. Nations.
Let the women rise.

Not above.
Not beneath.
But beside.

This is not a cultural trend.
This is Eden restored.

This is the "not good" of creation reversed.
This is the Kingdom breaking in.

So let it begin with us.

Let 'Ēzer Roar

Let her voice rise in homes.
Let her wisdom shape the Church.
Let her strength tear down injustice.
Let her courage birth revival.

She was never meant to shrink.
She was always meant to roar.

Postscript: Understanding Paul's Words About Women

What About Paul's Words?

Throughout this book, we've explored the fierce, God-given strength of *'ēzer*— women as rescuers, partners, image-bearers.

Some readers might wonder:
"But what about Paul's instructions about women in the church?"

Let's look together—
not with fear, but with faith that God's Word, rightly understood, never contradicts itself.

Ephesians 5: Submission and Love

Paul calls wives to submit to their husbands.
Yet he also commands husbands to lay down
their lives as Christ did.

This isn't domination—
it's mutual self-giving.

Submission here is not silence but a willing
partnership
shaped by love, never fear.

1 Timothy 2 and 1 Corinthians 14

These verses have been interpreted in many
ways.

Some see them as prohibitions for all times and
places.
Others understand them in their cultural con-
text—
specific instructions addressing disruptions in
worship
and untrained teaching in Ephesus and Corinth.

What's clear is this:
Paul also affirms women praying, prophesying, and leading.

He greets Junia, *"outstanding among the apostles."*
He praises Priscilla as a teacher.

The same Spirit who fell on sons and daughters still empowers all believers to build the Kingdom.

We don't erase these passages or dismiss them.
We hold them in tension,
always returning to the truth that in Christ,
we are co-heirs of grace.

God's design has never been hierarchy born of fear,
but harmony born of love.

So let your strength rise.
Let it roar.

If you'd like to explore this topic further, here are two excellent resources:

- *What Paul Really Said About Women* by John T. Bristow

- *The Christian Woman... Set Free: Women Freed from the Second-Class Citizenship in the Kingdom of God* by Gene Edwards

No matter where you begin, may you discover the freedom and courage God designed for you from the very beginning.

Other books by Christian A. Dickinson

I f you enjoyed *Roar of 'Ēzer*, you may also appreciate these Christ-centered resources:

FULL CIRCLE: PREGAME — A Devotional Series for Athletes

Before the whistle blows and the lights come up, PREGAME challenges athletes to prepare their hearts as well as their bodies. With powerful stories, Scripture reflections, and real talk from the locker room, Coach Dickinson and Anthony "Diso" Paradiso equip competitors to lead with faith, play with integrity, and honor Christ in every moment.

Jesus Was Funnier Than You Think: Unlocking His Wit, Wisdom, and Unexpected Humor

A fresh look at the wit and humor of Jesus Christ

— revealing the brilliant, joyful ways He taught truth and disarmed pride.

The Prophetic Equation: Thirty Prophets. One Christ. Zero Coincidence.

An exploration of how thirty prophetic voices across centuries, kingdoms, and crises converge with stunning precision in Jesus Christ — revealing that Scripture is not random, but a masterpiece of divine design.

Micah 6:8: A Prophetic Bridge to Jesus

A concise biblical commentary exploring how one ancient verse points forward to the life and ministry of Christ.

The Curse of Time: Time Began When Eternity Broke

A theological and personal exploration of time as a consequence of sin—not a neutral part of creation. Drawing from Scripture, Church Fathers, and moments of divine encounter, this book challenges the assumption that time was God's original design and invites readers to rediscover the eternal now of God's presence.

Every Tear Remembered: God's Presence in Our Grief

A reflection on sorrow, healing, and hope through the lens of God's enduring love.

It's All or Nothing: How Jesus Raised the Standard from Tithing to Full Surrender

A biblical commentary challenging traditional views of tithing by exploring Jesus' call to radical, Spirit-led generosity.

About the Author

Christian A. Dickinson is an author, educator, and speaker dedicated to exploring the intersection of faith, identity, and purpose. With over two decades of experience as a teacher, coach, and school leader, Christian has mentored countless students and families, helping them discover the transformative power of biblical truth.

He holds a deep conviction that God's design for humanity includes the unique, courageous calling of women as image bearers—warriors, nurturers, and leaders empowered by the Spirit. In *The Roar of 'Ēzer*, Christian draws from Scripture, history, and personal stories to illu-

minate the strength and dignity of women created as'ēzer—helpers who stand shoulder to
shoulder with men in God's mission.

Christian is the author of a cadre of biblical
commentary books, devotionals for athletes,
and children's picture books. He is married to
his'ēzer, Morgan, and they have four children.